MW00593250

Youth Event @ 2pm!

KEEP THIS COUPON

TICKET

THE SKINNY

ON

VOLUNTEERS

Hello!

Jonathan McKee

with Danette Matty

Group

JESUS–
CENTERED

Guide your entire ministry
toward a passionate
Jesus-centered focus with
this series of innovative
resources. Harness the
power of these dynamic
tools that will help you draw
teenagers and leaders into a
closer orbit around Jesus.

The Skinny on Volunteers
© 2015 Jonathan McKee

group.com
simplyyouthministry.com

Credits
Authors: Jonathan McKee with Danette Matty
Executive Developer: Tim Gilmour
Executive Editor: Rick Lawrence
Chief Creative Officer: Joani Schultz
Editor: Rob Cunningham
Art Director and Cover Art: Veronica Preston
Cover Photography: Rodney Stewart
Production: Joyce Douglas
Project Manager: Stephanie Krajec

Unless otherwise indicated, Scripture quotations are taken from the Holy Bible,
New Living Translation, copyright ©1996, 2004, 2007, 2013 by Tyndale House
Foundation. Used by permission of Tyndale House Publishers, Inc., Carol Stream,
Illinois 60188. All rights reserved.

Scripture quotations marked NIV are taken from THE HOLY BIBLE, NEW
INTERNATIONAL VERSION®, NIV® Copyright © 1973, 1978, 1984, 2011 by Biblica,
Inc.™ Used by permission. All rights reserved worldwide.

Any website addresses included in this book are offered only as a resource and/or
reference for the reader. The inclusion of these websites are not intended, in any
way, to be interpreted as an endorsement of these sites or their content on the part of
Group Publishing or the author. In addition, the author and Group Publishing do not
vouch for the content of these websites for the life of this book.

ISBN 978-1-4707-2085-8
10 9 8 7 6 5 4 3 2 1   21 20 19 18 17 16 15

Printed in the United States of America.

ACKNOWLEDGMENTS

Thanks to Jesus my Lord, who is the source of anything good that comes out of me, and who I'd be lost without.

Thanks to my family for putting up with me while writing this book. When I finished this project, Ashley shouted, "Good, we can have the living room back!" (Yes, our most comfy chair is in our living room!)

A huge shoutout to my blog readers at JonathanMcKeeWrites.com for this book. When I finished a draft on a Friday, I asked if anyone would like to read it over the weekend and offer their "two cents," and I had a phenomenal response. So a huge thanks especially to Corey Speer, Jeff Dempsey, Sharon Schultz, Kevin Downey, Jono Davis, Kyle Bueermann, Jared Callis, Dan Davis, Matthew Erickson, Lisa Burris, Ramona Gramly, Kenneth Taylor, Jordan Spivey, Sharon Hannaby, Nick Mance, Lou Jordan, Kathie Barkow, Rob Vande Lune, Kyle Wassom, JT Toler, Jake Bartkovsky, Dan Neighbors, David Brinkley, Chad Feight, and Jenn Chen.

I also have to thank my friend Danette Matty for working with me on this project. Danette and I worked together years ago; it was so good to work together again.

And always a big thanks to my agent and friend Greg Johnston!

— **Jonathan McKee**

THE SKINNY

ON

VOLUNTEERS

CONTENTS

THE SKINNY ON

VOLUNTEERS

BEFORE YOU GET STARTED

The book you're holding might be "skinny," but that's because it's all-muscle. This means that Jonathan McKee and Danette Matty have cut away the fat and focused on the "first things" that make volunteer leadership in youth ministry powerful and long-lasting. In our Skinny Books series, we've paired a thought leader (in this case, Jonathan McKee) with a master practitioner (in this case, Danette Matty) as a one-two punch. We want you to be challenged and equipped in both your thinking and your doing.

And, as a bonus, we've added an Introduction written by Kurt Johnston and Katie Edwards that explores volunteer leadership through the filter of a Jesus-centered approach to ministry. Jesus-centered is much more than a catchphrase to us—it's a passionate and transformative approach to life and ministry. Kurt and Katie's Introduction to volunteers first appeared in my book *Jesus-Centered Youth Ministry,* and we couldn't think of a better way to kick off this little book. It's time to get skinny...

—RICK LAWRENCE
Executive Editor of Group Magazine

THE SKINNY ON

VOLUNTEERS

INTRODUCTION

Jesus was the first person in the church to develop a team of volunteers to help him fulfill his ministry call. Jesus had lots to do and a short time to do it. He and his ragtag group of disciples forged a unique team that changed the world.

The two of us have partnered in youth ministry together for almost 20 years—two decades of summer camps, surf outings, mission trips, and memories. We've learned a *whole lot* of youth ministry lessons, but one that we've been reminded about over and over again is that youth ministry really couldn't happen without a team of adult volunteers.

One of the first things Jesus did when he began his public ministry was to build a team to help out. Youth ministry is a fast-paced, stress-filled, never-ending job. It's tempting to focus on the tasks at hand (planning the next event, writing the next lesson, T.P.-ing the next house) and overlook the most important task: building a team to make an eternal difference. Let's learn from Jesus' example...

1. **Jesus enlisted.** Jesus didn't sit around and hope that what he was about to do would attract people to his cause. Instead, he enlisted others to join his team. He made "the ask" in a compelling way. In Matthew 4:19, when he said to Peter and Andrew, "Come, follow me, and I will show you how to fish for people," imagine how compelling that

must have sounded to two young men who made their living being fishers of fish!

2. **Jesus equipped.** Jesus knew the stakes were high. In just a few years, his little team of fishermen, doctors, and doubters would have to continue his work. So instead of spending time lecturing them with fill-in-the-blank training sessions, he equipped them by giving them a whole lot of on-the-job training.

3. **Jesus empowered.** As Jesus equipped his leaders, he also empowered them. He encouraged Peter's bold proclamation by encouraging him to walk on water! When the disciples shared their concern that the multitudes listening to him teach were getting hungry, he said, "You give them something to eat" (Mark 6:37, NIV). Before he ascended into heaven, he empowered them with the Holy Spirit and reminded them of the task at hand.

Jesus chose to partner with those who loved him to expand his Father's kingdom—he enlisted, equipped, and empowered others to play a crucial role in his redemptive mission. He certainly *could* have done it all on his own, but because relationship is paramount to him, he decided to partner...with us.

—Kurt Johnston, *Director of Student Ministries at Saddleback Church*

—Katie Edwards, *Junior High Pastor at Saddleback Church*

CHAPTER

1

Which

Is

Better?

THE SKINNY VOLUNTEERS

Two different youth ministries, two different states, both from similar-sized churches with comparable budgets, both in the month of September. One ministry was fizzling out and struggling, and the other was booming.

The difference?

A leader who valued volunteers.

Honestly, ask yourself: Which is better?

> A. A magnetic, relational youth leader who loves hanging out with kids.
>
> B. A solid youth leader who can recruit 20 to 30 relational volunteers who *each* love hanging out with kids.

All other factors being equal, which would you rather have? Who would you rather be?

As I visited these two churches, it became very evident what kind of leader each church had hired.

THE TEXAS LONE RANGER

The first was a church of about 1,000 in Texas. The youth pastor was sharp, educated, and looked just a hair too much like Channing Tatum. He brought me out to speak at one of his events.

When he first called me I asked him, "Would you like me to do some training with your team while I'm there? It's no extra cost. I'm happy to do any of my workshops while ya got me there."

"Thanks," he replied. "I actually have that handled. But we're super excited for you to speak at our Battle of the Bands event!"

I'll never forget my dinner with this guy before the event. He was frustrated with his ministry on several levels:

1. He had 30-40 teenagers coming to his program each week, but he felt like they were just slipping in and out. They weren't connecting with anyone.

2. He had a number of kids who needed to be discipled. He was running a Bible study where he was trying to disciple them all at once, but the study was chaotic and often wandered off onto tangents.

3. He was out too many nights and was spread too thin.

4. He felt like his senior pastor wasn't supportive, especially in the area of budget. This youth pastor wanted to hire a bunch of interns to expand his ministry, but the senior pastor insisted on using volunteers.

Frankly, every problem he shared with me was something that pointed to his need for a team of volunteers who would love kids, connect with them, and disciple them.

He had three volunteers—*including his wife*.

We finished dinner and dived into the Battle of the Bands. His event brought out about 45 kids. It was unorganized and out of control.

I heard he left the church a year later.

THE WICHITA TEAM

The second church was in Wichita, Kansas—another church of about 1,000. The church hired my dad and me to come out and train leaders to be better at recruiting and retaining volunteers. We arrived the night before and peeked in on an outreach event in the gym.

Our jaws almost dropped to the floor. The church was almost the exact same size as the Texas church, but we were looking at over 150 middle schoolers filling a gymnasium. And as I looked around the room, I counted almost 40 volunteers hanging out with kids, laughing and interacting.

We'd never seen so many volunteers!

As we talked with the youth pastor later that evening, he told us, "We are so excited to have you guys here to train us. We really have a lot to learn about volunteers."

My dad and I looked at each other like, *Really? Because it looks like we are the ones who should be taking notes here!*

One guy—who desperately needed some training—didn't want any training. He "had it handled."

And his ministry was suffering.

The other guy—who was doing an amazing job—humbly wanted to do it even better.

And God was doing amazing things through this ministry.

Which one are you?

THE HARVEST

Ministry was booming.

Jesus had healed a paralyzed dude, a leper, and some blind guys, and had cast out a bunch of demons. He had even brought a girl back from the dead (that one got everyone talking). When he wasn't healing, he was teaching or just hanging out with the people who gathered to meet him.

Wherever Jesus went, crowds followed. Ministry was thriving.

In the middle of this exciting ministry, Jesus paused. He looked out across the crowds who had gathered, and as he stared into the eyes of the people standing before him, *his heart broke for them.*

> *"When he saw the crowds, he had compassion on them because they were confused and helpless, like sheep without a shepherd. He said to his disciples, 'The harvest is great, but the workers are few. So pray to the Lord who is in charge of the harvest; ask him to send more workers into his fields'" (Matthew 9:36-38).*

Even the Messiah acknowledged the need for more workers.

Have you?

More importantly: *Have you taken his advice?*

Seriously. I'm not asking a rhetorical question. I really want you to think for a moment. Have you ever come to Jesus with a broken heart and prayed for workers?

Specifically, when you look out at the people of your community and see the potential to make a difference, do you think, "Wait, I'd love to do that, but I don't have enough workers."

Did you bring that to Jesus? Have you ever prayed this kind of prayer night after night?

> *"This ministry has amazing potential to thrive. I daily see kids who need positive mentors. I encounter student leaders who are ready to be discipled. I just need more help! Please help me find workers for this ministry."*

Sometimes we forget to take Jesus up on this. We forget to ask for his help.

Sadly, if we're being realistic, most of us don't do much when it comes to mobilizing volunteers and equipping them for ministry. Don't take my word for it; just do a quick inventory of your hours this week:

1. How much time did you spend brainstorming or thinking about who would be great leaders in your ministry?

2. How much time did you spend talking with these potential volunteers, or "pre-volunteers" as I like to call them?

3. How much time did you spend equipping, encouraging, or building into your existing volunteers?

I spend a lot of time with youth workers. And the majority of youth workers don't tally even one hour a week in those activities.

Some of you are saying, "But Jonathan, this is hard! Where can I fit this into my already overstuffed calendar?"

I hear you, and I relate. If you're like me, your plate is already full, and this sounds like yet another task to add to the list.

But what if the efforts you put into mobilizing and equipping volunteers would actually lighten your schedule? What if this investment of time actually paid back double, quadruple, or even tenfold?

Would you do it then?

I'm not going to lie to you. No matter how you slice it, our initial investment into mobilizing volunteers takes time. But think of the alternative...

VOLUNTEER MATH

Let's do a little math.

If you look at the time you spend each week with teenagers, you could go out there and spend 20 hours a week with students by yourself.

> *You put in 20 hours and reap 20 hours of impact.*
>
> *20 = 20*

Or you could take that same block of time, spend 10 hours with students, and 10 hours a week developing 10 volunteers so that they eventually can EACH spend 5 volunteer hours (50 hours total) a week with students. That's 60.

> *You put in 20 hours and reap 60 hours of impact.*
>
> *20 = 60*

This model isn't just good math; it's scriptural. Jesus devoted time to the crowds, but he also spent time developing the Twelve (Matthew 4:18-22; Matthew 10), not to mention the 70+ regulars who were also gleaning from his teaching (Luke 10)—probably the same group from which they chose Judas' replacement (Acts 1). These guys not only helped Jesus while he was here on earth, they also continued his ministry when he was gone.

Think what this might look like in your ministry.

What if you developed teachers who saved you weekly prep time? What if you recruited office help who did many of the logistical tasks you get buried in? What if you trained leaders who would launch entire ministries without you?

Or you could just do it all yourself.

HOW DO WE DO IT?

For most of us, the question isn't *if* we want volunteers— the question is *how* we get them and keep them.

In this little book, we're going to concentrate on three simple skills that will help you mobilize and equip leaders for the work of the harvest: *recruiting, keeping,* and *training* volunteers.

Let's dig in. And we'll start by talking about *recruiting...*

⊙ A VOLUNTEER'S PERSPECTIVE *Danette Matty*

I love "Would you rather?" discussion questions—silly stuff like, "Would you rather be seen picking your nose or throwing up?" As a volunteer, the question is, "Would I rather show up at youth group and hope to make a difference, or spend time with my youth pastor learning how to make a difference?" I'm smart and self-motivated, but I don't know it all. And with the exponential pace youth culture changes, I'm still growing as a leader. I want to be great at leading youth, so I want my youth pastor's voice of experience and input.

A monthly meeting is essential for sharing vision and strategy with your team, and getting group feedback from them. But for developing your sharpest leaders, carve out a couple of hours at a convenient time—maybe a Saturday morning every two months—and meet with volunteers in 45-minute increments. That's not a lot of time, but when my youth leader did it for me, it was 45 minutes of focused face time. My youth leader would ask me how I was doing personally, and we'd discuss that for 15-20 minutes. And then we'd talk about my role in our ministry, meshing the ministry vision with my strengths.

More than one youth pastor has said, "If volunteers didn't do their jobs, I couldn't do mine." When I know you genuinely care about me, I care more about you and your ministry.

CHAPTER 2

Recruiting

Volunteers

THE SKINNY ON

VOLUNTEERS

Kent had been a youth pastor for seven years when I met with him, but he was discouraged and had begun looking at other vocations.

"Why so glum?" I asked him directly.

His ministry seemed fruitful. Kids were meeting Jesus for the first time, and Christ-followers were getting to know Jesus better. On a typical week about 40 to 50 teenagers would come to his midweek youth group, and he interacted with even more on campus several times a month. I didn't see any reason to be gloomy.

"No one wants to help," Kent said. "I have so many opportunities, and so few workers."

"Been there!" I assured him. In fact, I think most youth workers tend to float in that same boat.

So I asked him the "money" question:

"So who have you asked?"

He paused and looked at me like I had said something taboo. Sadly, I wasn't surprised. I've seen that look many times. I almost expect it, in fact.

"Well," he stammered, "we did an announcement in church, but no one responded."

Kent was a friend and I didn't want to make him feel stupid, but I also didn't want him to quit his job over something that didn't have to be a problem. So I probed a little deeper. "Forget announcements—*who have you asked?* Who have you literally walked up to in the last year, in person, and asked them to join your team?"

Silence.

This conversation has happened more times than I can count.

SIMPLY ASK PEOPLE

In the last decade I've had the privilege of seeing hundreds of youth ministries firsthand—groups of 5 and groups of 500. I speak at churches, events, or camps about twice a month. So I've had plenty of opportunities to sit with youth pastors and volunteer leaders, listening to them each share their heart about their ministry.

Whenever the subject of volunteers is brought up, I always notice a couple of common denominators:

1. Churches never have enough volunteers. I rarely meet a youth worker who's just busting at the seams with volunteers—99 percent of churches would welcome more workers. Wouldn't you?

2. Regardless of the need, ministry leaders rarely make personal face-to-face invitations to become part of the ministry.

This little book could save you a ton of time and energy, because I'm about to provide you with the simple secret to getting more volunteers.

Are you ready? This one simple practice will change your ministry.

Here it is...

ASK!

Yeah. It really is that simple.

I promise you—it works!

Just a couple of years ago when my youngest daughter was in junior high, my wife and I volunteered in our church's middle school ministry. My travel took me out of town several weekends a month, but I rarely traveled midweek. So when the opportunity to be a small group leader emerged, I jumped at the chance. (I love middle school kids!)

My friend Chris was the youth pastor. He loves kids and is really gifted relationally. Chris could hear a kid's name once and remember it the following week. His memory and personal skills astounded me. Chris would also visit each of them at their sporting events throughout the year. Chris made kids feel special.

But there was only one Chris.

Chris had a handful of volunteers, but not enough. Take Wednesday nights, for example. The format was simple. He'd always have some fun activity, then he'd kick off discussion with a story or a video, and then students would get into small groups.

The format worked. Teenagers not only had fun, but they also felt noticed and heard in their small groups each week. The discussions were real and relevant, and they always pointed to the Bible. Maybe that's why the group seemed to grow in numbers. Small groups started with five or six kids in each group but then grew to eight or more.

Week after week I'd hear other small group leaders say what I was thinking: "It's cool that the groups are growing, but maybe we can add some groups so we can keep things to a manageable size." (I'm a big advocate of keeping small groups about four to eight kids—a good range to provoke good discussion, while not making anyone feel ignored.)

Each week Chris would respond the same way. "Yeah, if we had more leaders, but we don't. So let's just keep loving the kids we got."

I loved Chris' positive spirit. He wasn't going to let a lack of volunteers get him down. But did he need to settle for "a lack of volunteers"?

Finally, one week I just asked him: "Chris, have you asked some others about volunteering?"

You can probably guess his reply:

> *"Well, we announced it at church, and..."*

I interrupted. "Have you pulled anyone aside and just asked them, face to face?"

Chris was always completely honest. "No, not really. I just feel...*awkward*."

So I asked him, "I actually know a few couples who I think would be really good—would you like me to ask them for you?"

We brainstormed for about three minutes and I walked away committing to ask six people.

The next week, two of them checked it out. The following week, another one showed up. All three of them ended up helping for the next couple of years.

I'm not going to lie and tell you that six people said yes. As a matter of fact, three people said no.

But three people said yes!

We're never going to get volunteers if we don't ask! Most people just rely on announcements and emails and wonder why no one ever comes knocking. But we have to ask.

VOLUNTEER ISN'T A VERB

This is really a problem of grammar. We need to think of *volunteer* as a noun, not as a verb. People don't want to *volunteer*; they want to be asked.

My dad, creator of VolunteerPower.com, tells the story of an experience as a senior pastor when he was putting together a building committee. The church had a project that needed to be accomplished. Frankly, he didn't want just anyone handling this; he wanted Bill. Bill owned a successful construction company for decades and was the perfect project leader for this team.

On a Sunday morning, my dad mentioned the project and announced that he was looking for volunteers to complete this important task. A week went by...

Nothing.

Finally, as the next week rolled in, my dad called up Bill and admitted, "I really was thinking of you for that project. I was hoping you'd *volunteer*."

My dad always shares, "That was my mistake. I thought the word *volunteer* was a verb."

Bill told my dad candidly, "I'd be happy to do the project. Why didn't you just ask?"

My dad was excited to have Bill on the project, but he was even more intrigued by a peripheral comment Bill said:

> *"I've volunteered for stuff before, and it was always a waste of my time. I don't volunteer anymore. If you want something, ask me."*

That incident changed the way my dad recruited, and it molded the way I recruit, too. In fact, I recently took on a project for my home church to totally revamp a room where we were launching a ministry to parents.

The budget was literally $0, but we needed electrical, multimedia, a little bit of construction, and interior design.

I called up my buddy Todd, who knew electrical; my buddy Scott, the multimedia guru; my friend Steve, who had his own construction company; and my friend Anita, who has better design sense than all of us. All of these people are parents and were excited about this ministry, so when I told them the plans, they were happy to participate.

After a few more phone calls raising the money, we literally pounded out the needed remodel in one weekend.

I never made one announcement.

I simply sat down, made a list of my dream team, and called them up individually and said, "I want you, and here's why."

People want to be needed.

People want to make a difference.

People want to be asked!

⊙ A VOLUNTEER'S PERSPECTIVE *Danette Matty*

I'm a fan of asking people to help for a specified time period and/or a specific role or project. Specific questions get specific answers.

Instead of asking, "Can you hang with teenagers on Wednesday nights?" ask, "Will you help Gina serve concessions before and after youth group the first and third Wednesday of each month until the end of the semester (or end of the school year)?"

Instead of saying, "I need group leaders," say, "I'd like to pair you with another youth worker to lead a small group for high school guys. We're asking each small group leader to facilitate a group every week during the semester or every other week through the end of the school year. Would either work for your schedule?"

HOW DO I ASK?

Some of you are saying, "Jonathan, I've tried! I've asked people and they always say no! Is it my body odor? Why can't I get more volunteers?"

Don't worry; you're not alone. Sometimes our lack of volunteers isn't because we don't ask; it's because of *how* we ask.

I've been in youth ministry for over two decades, and during that time I've noticed three distinct ways we shoot ourselves in the foot when recruiting volunteers. Do everything possible to avoid these three "fails."

FAIL #1: YOU'RE ASKING THE WRONG PEOPLE

I was speaking at a church in Wisconsin recently, and the Sunday I preached was the first Sunday for a new children's director. They interviewed her in the services, giving people a chance to get to know her, and in both services she made an awkward announcement: "I encourage you to come and see me and let me know if you can help in the nursery this month. As you know, we could always use nursery workers."

Churches love to make announcements.

In our book *The New Breed,* my dad and I go into great detail about the common pitfalls of recruiting, including the Seven Sins of Recruiting. Our first sin: *Expect announcements to get volunteers!*

I'm not saying to never do announcements. They can serve as good marketing. They can raise awareness to a need. Sometimes they can even garner a few volunteers.

Here's the problem with *relying* on announcements:

1. Announcements rarely get a good response.

2. Announcements often collect the wrong people.

And a bad volunteer is sometimes worse than no volunteer at all.

So how do you avoid getting the wrong volunteer?

First, make a list of your "dream team."

DREAM TEAM

I've done this on several occasions. Perhaps the most memorable time was when I went to work one day and found a folder from my boss, with a sticky note that read, "This is now yours."

I had inherited a middle school ministry that someone else had run down to almost zilch, nada—nothing. I had been directing high school and some other responsibilities up to that point, but my job description suddenly doubled over the weekend.

If only my paycheck had doubled!

The group had just a handful of kids and about four volunteers. Then two volunteers departed when the other guy left, so I was left with just two.

This ministry had the potential to reach hundreds, and I knew that two volunteers wouldn't cut it. So I started from scratch. I sat down and prayed, "God, please send me workers for my harvest." I asked God specifically to help me as I gathered these workers. "Bring people to mind."

And God did. So I began to write names for my "dream team." These were the people I wanted—friends who I knew would be good mentors and had a heart for ministry. A couple of them had worked in youth ministry before; many of them hadn't. But they all loved Jesus and were willing to serve.

Don't limit yourself to who *you think* are best. Let God bring you people. I always end up with other names on my list through referrals and word of mouth. Sometimes God brings people we would have never thought of.

My final list had about 15 names on it. I eventually recruited about 10 of them.

But how is this done? By giving them just a "taste" of the ministry. And that leads me to the second "fail" that can mess up our recruiting efforts...

➲ A VOLUNTEER'S PERSPECTIVE *Danette Matty*

I C N U—letters that can help you lead with what you see in people when you're recruiting volunteers. I see in you...

> "I see how you talk with young people. You look them in the eye. You laugh easily. You ask them questions before you talk about yourself."

> "I see how faithful you are around here, and I wonder if there's untapped leadership in you."

> "I see your attention to detail when you're working on something."

And after you tell me in one or two sentences what you see in me, tell me how I'd be a fit for your team.

> "You'd be a great small group leader."

> "I'd like someone dependable in the tech booth during worship and the teaching time."

> "I can see you influencing student leaders and helping pull out their strengths."

If you communicate that you want me to be myself and care in tangible ways about a couple of kids and/or one specific area of ministry, I'm confident I can handle that.

FAIL #2: YOU ASK FOR MARRIAGE INSTEAD OF A DATE

I told my wife, Lori, I was going to marry her on the first weekend we dated. She broke up with me one week later.

Looking back, I don't blame her. I was 20, waaaaaaaaaaay too intense, and far too ignorant to keep my mouth shut about how I felt. So when Lori captured my heart, I made a huge mistake: *I told her exactly how I felt.*

Guys, *never* do this!

Women don't want to hear that you are madly in love with them after one or two dates. This is not the way to court a woman. You don't walk up and say, "I've never seen such beauty. I'm truly captivated. You are the one, and I mean 'The One!' This is love—as in 'you, me, 2.6 children, a white-picket fence, and a Labrador' love. Don't deny it. Let's get a preacher and make this official!"

This isn't the way to date, and it's not the way to recruit volunteers. Don't ask for marriage instead of a date.

But we do this all the time.

"Hey, Greg. What are you doing on Wednesdays, Sundays, and weekends? Because I'm looking for someone to spend time with teenagers every Wednesday night for the next year, plus Sundays, plus a bunch of crazy weekends, including a few all-nighters (I hope you like pizza, caffeine, and Xanax), plus a week of camp in Houston this summer—oh, and a painfully boring one-day training that is required for all volunteers, and a background check to make sure you aren't some pedophile. Soooo...wanna join up?"

FAIL!

So how should we ask Greg?

Try this:

"Greg, next Saturday, 30 middle school kids are showing up to serve in the community. We're going to rake leaves, visit a rest home, feed homeless at the Salvation Army, and paint an elderly neighbor's house. I really need a driver who could help us with the painting team, and I know you used to paint houses. Would you like to join us? I could really use your help?"

You're not asking for marriage...*just a "date."*

Think about the logic behind this. You're not asking Greg to clear his calendar for the next year. You're asking for one day.

You're not asking Greg to do something painful or foreign. You're asking him to do something he's good at.

⊖ A VOLUNTEER'S PERSPECTIVE *Danette Matty*

Look for people who have a growing relationship with Jesus and who genuinely care about teenagers. If I'm recruiting, I sometimes say, "I don't need a rock star or a social worker. I just need someone who genuinely likes teenagers—and they can tell if you do or don't. I want someone who will choose one or two kids to talk to every week, in person, by phone, by social media, or by text. Find out what they're into, show up to their school events now and then, and pray for them regularly."

If you believe I'd make a good youth worker and can tell me why (I C N U), you can show me the value of investing in teenagers with stories of their lives and why they're worth my time and love.

FIRST "DATE"

Years ago I needed volunteers desperately for a campus ministry I had developed. We had about 200 students coming out to a school gym each Thursday night, and I only had 12 volunteers.

Don't get me wrong: That was *great* when I had about 40 kids. But with 200, we had groups of 17 or 18 with each leader!

So I called up my friend Jenny and said, "Jenny, I really need your help. This coming Thursday night, I'm having a root beer float event at the school. It's a great opportunity, we have a couple hundred kids coming out each week because they've got nothing else to do, and we get a chance to put positive role models in their lives and share the gospel each week. Anyway, I really need someone who can help me just scoop ice cream and make root beer floats this week so I can free up my adult leaders to hang out with kids and build relationships with them."

I emphasized the simplicity of it. "Could I get you to help us this once?"

Jenny gladly accepted my invitation. And when she showed up that night to help, I made time to stop and talk with her several times throughout the evening, thanking her and telling her a little more about the ministry. I would point out a particular teenager and tell Jenny a little of the kid's life story. Jenny stuck around and saw me talking about Jesus. She saw kids respond and get Bibles.

That night Jenny got a "taste" of what the ministry was all about, and I specifically thanked her for serving and giving my team the opportunity to build into the lives of kids. Many of our volunteers thanked her as well.

As she left I told her, "You were an awesome help. Let's talk more this week."

I didn't try to "close the sale." I simply asked her for a second "date."

SECOND "DATE"

That week I brought another volunteer along, and we met Jenny for coffee. We thanked her again for her help and spent most of the time answering her questions about the ministry. She even asked us about my existing volunteers.

"So all those college kids and adults—do they come help you every week?"

"Yep," I explained. "Every one of them started helping in a small way, but they eventually decided to become one of our regular volunteer leaders. They've each been checked, fingerprinted, and interviewed—a small hoop to jump through to provide safety and protection for everyone."

Notice that the "dating" process doesn't require us to lower our standards; it just requires us to pace ourselves so we don't scare people away. We can—and should— maintain high standards with our volunteers.

The same is probably true with our normal dating relationships, right? We *don't* have to settle for less just because we decided we *won't* rush into relationships.

That's why we eventually take volunteers through our normal screening process, which needs to include elements like fingerprinting or background checks.

And I'm not afraid to mention those standards to potential volunteers on the second or third "date."

After our lunch together, I didn't ask Jenny to sign on the bottom line—I just asked her to come again.

In fact, I said, "Next week is going to be a little different. No root beer floats, no big program. In fact, we divide into small groups. Want to come and sit in on one?"

Jenny said yes and visited our ministry again—*and she was hooked*. I practically didn't even have to ask her to become one of my regular volunteers. She asked me!

All because of that first "date": *Can you come and scoop ice cream?*

Jenny became one of our weekly volunteers. In fact, she is still a friend today and a supporter of our ministry.

Don't ask for marriage. Just get a "date."

Find an opportunity to invite someone from your "dream team" out to get a positive "taste" of your ministry. Don't ask them to sign on the bottom line; just ask them to come again.

After two or three "dates," you can let them know more about your ministry needs and find a place where they can make a difference.

Sometimes, they might say no. And if they do, that's OK.

In fact, you might want to be careful of the third "fail" so common when recruiting...

FAIL #3: YOU'RE ASSUMING "NO" MEANS "NEVER"

When someone tells us no, what else might he or she be saying?

"No" rarely means, *"Don't ever ask me again!"* It typically means...

- "Not now"

- "Not that particular task"

- "Not on that evening"

- "Not with that group"

"No" can mean a lot of things, but it rarely means "never."

Like when I first asked my friend TJ to help with my middle school ministry. TJ told me no. He said the word *no*, but I didn't realize he meant "not now."

Years later his friend Quincy was volunteering with our ministry. Quincy said, "I should ask my friend TJ to help out each week." (It's a great recruiting tool, by the way, when your volunteers recruiting their friends!)

I, being young and naïve, said, "Oh, don't bother. I already asked TJ. He said no."

Quincy, being young and wise, asked TJ anyway.

Guess what TJ said?

"Yes."

"No" doesn't always mean "never."

I'm not saying that you have to become one of those pushy used car salesman who doesn't take no for an answer. Recruiting volunteers is different from sales—

we're not convincing them to buy something or do something. In fact, we're trying to find people with a passion for ministry and give them an opportunity to use their gifts.

"Guilting" techniques don't work. You may harness someone who works a few times, but you won't be finding a long-term volunteer.

The key to discovering this is *listening*.

Good leaders of volunteers are good listeners. They listen at every stage of the recruiting process. They listen to the potential volunteer's passions and concerns.

Today's volunteers are busy, they're particular, and they don't want their time wasted. If we don't listen to our potential volunteers, we'll never match them to a position that fits their personality, skills, and gifting.

* * *

It all starts with asking.

Have you sat down and made a list of your "dream team"?

Have you prayed over this list? Maybe God has some people in mind that you didn't think of.

Have you looked for good opportunities for "first dates" where you can give these potential volunteers a "taste" of your ministry?

Have you listened to their passions and concerns and found a good fit for them to use their gifts in your ministry?

This is all part of recruiting.

But now we face a key question: How do you keep your volunteers? Let's spend some time talking about this...

THE SKINNY ON

VOLUNTEERS

CHAPTER 3

Keeping

Volunteers

THE SKINNY *ON*

VOLUNTEERS

My next-door neighbor spent over $30,000 putting in a new yard. The project took three months, and after all that work with cement contractors, fence builders, and landscapers, his yard looked perfect with its brand-new plants and fresh, green sod. The end result was fabulous—*for about three days.*

A new lawn needs *extra water* the first few weeks; if not, the grass will never take root and will start to brown on the edges, eventually withering and dying.

My neighbor didn't understand what extra water meant, because within 24 hours I saw the edges of each roll starting to look dry. By day two, the edges were so dry that dead stripes were appearing throughout the yard. By day three, his yard was in triage.

Why spend so much time and effort putting something in place only to neglect it once it's there?

I see it happen in the volunteer world all the time.

In fact, I've seen organizations that are phenomenal at recruiting but have disastrous retention numbers. Some of these organizations just write it off as typical volunteer attrition. If they lose 80 percent of their new volunteer workforce? "Who cares—at least we're 20 percent better than before."

This is silly. If I recruit my dream team, I'd prefer to *keep* my dream team, rather than having to constantly work to refill my bench! *Keeping* volunteers is just as important as *recruiting* volunteers.

So what's the secret? Here are five elements I always provide for my dream team:

1. TIME

Near the beginning of this book, we did the math. We can spend 20 hours hanging out with teenagers each week, or we can spend 10 hours hanging with kids and another 10 investing in some volunteers who will *each* spend 5 hours a week with a kid. (I choose the latter.)

Think what this might look like in your ministry. How can you build into your volunteers?

I used to block out a weekly breakfast for several of my volunteer guys. This was a great time to ask them how they were doing, to encourage them, and to even talk a little about ministry. This time was vital because on Thursday nights, we were busy investing in teenagers. These morning times gave me a chance to disciple these leaders and gave them the opportunity to bond with each other.

⊙ A VOLUNTEER'S PERSPECTIVE *Danette Matty*

It can be intimidating for a new volunteer to show up, stand around, and wonder what to do while established team members confidently buzz around them. Most new youth workers feel they need permission to do something before they're confident that it's "their place."

In the youth ministry I serve, we asked two established youth workers—one from the middle school team and one from the high school team—to each be our Assimilation Connect person. (Sounds all "cyborgish," but we haven't come up with a cooler title. Don't judge.)

They attend our quarterly New Youth Worker Orientation, meet the newly minted team members, and get their contact info. Their job for the next three weeks is to go out of their way at youth group to connect with the new volunteers.

They make the new volunteers feel welcome and introduce them to students and other youth workers.

They allow the new volunteers to ask questions about how and why we do certain things.

And they encourage our newest team members as they settle into their own youth ministry groove.

My friend Greg was a youth worker at a large church 10 minutes from my house, and he had a similar practice to build into his 30+ volunteers. Each week he spent two mornings at our local family breakfast restaurant. During this time, if his volunteer youth leaders dropped by, Greg would pay for their meal. (It's nice to have the budget for this sort of thing.) Greg had regulars each time, plus a few who would come on occasion. His team members knew this was their time, and they would use it often.

Breakfasts, golfing, exercising, dinners—regardless of how you do it, investing in your volunteers will multiply into the lives of students.

And that takes time. But it also takes...

2. COMMUNICATION

You'd think communication would be easy when people are walking around with a Swiss Army Knife of technology in their pockets.

Yet, somehow, today's volunteers consistently complain about the lack of communication from leadership.

"That's ridiculous!" we say. "I send out a weekly five-page email briefing them on everything they need to know."

Email? Really?

Communication is vital, and communication preferences can be just as important.

Have you bought an airline ticket recently? When you do, most carriers will ask how you would like to be contacted: *email, phone,* or *text?* Everyone under age 35 chooses *text* (except that one guy on your team named Buford, who doesn't have a phone—but he's a different story). Everyone over 50 chooses *email.*

I'm not saying we shouldn't have volunteers older than 50; I'm just saying we need to learn how our volunteers communicate.

A June 2014 article in The New York Times (nytimes. com/2014/06/15/fashion/millennials-shy-away-from-voice-mail.html?_r=2) revealed that only 14 percent of young people actually even use a landline each day. Most delete voice mails without even listening to them. I've heard it from countless Millennials—those born between 1980 and the mid-1990s, roughly 20 to 35 years old at the time this book was released—"Don't even bother leaving a voice mail. I don't check them."

So what's the solution? Simply ask your volunteers their communication preference. Give them three choices for quick updates—maybe *Email, Text,* or *Social Media.* Use each person's preference for distributing quick, need-to-know information.

> *"Remember, this Thursday we're all bringing a basket of strawberries, a stapler, and a picture of our mother. The discussion will be on Proverbs, Chapter 5."*

In addition, if you like to provide small group questions for everyone, post them on a social media page and then use people's communication preference to send them the link.

➲ A VOLUNTEER'S PERSPECTIVE *Danette Matty*

After an informal interview and a cleared background check, your very next meeting with a new volunteer should be a fun, welcoming, informative orientation. Share your expectations for team members and what they can expect from you. This can be as short as 30 minutes at a coffee shop, or as long as 60 minutes in a conference room. Don't overwhelm them with your three-year strategy. Just share your overall vision, heart, and mission.

And don't make this the last meeting with your new volunteer. Some leaders do this one meeting and nothing else! Treat your volunteers like leaders from the beginning and make leadership development an ongoing priority.

Don't limit yourself to being digital. Connect with them in person. Keep all your volunteer leaders' numbers on speed dial on your phone and call them on the way home from seminary class, the grocery store, or the gym. Occasionally send them handwritten thank you notes to remind them that they're appreciated.

Whatever the method, keep in touch with your volunteers, know what's going on in their lives, and provide them an avenue of communication so they can stay current with the ministry.

One of the greatest places to communicate is at...

3. MORE THAN JUST A LEADERS' MEETING

I know, I know. The word *meeting* can draw whines and groans from volunteers. I understand. I'm not a big fan of meetings either. But it's important to have some sort of regular gathering with our team of leaders from time to time for needed updates, bonding, team-building, and a little bit of training (which we'll talk about in detail in the next chapter).

How often do you need these? That's up to you. Personally, I think weekly is a little much, but once a quarter isn't enough. So I encourage gathering leaders for some needed "team time" once a month.

I loved bringing together my middle school leadership team on Sunday nights. We switched off houses each month, which worked out well because we had about a dozen of us on the team, so we each ended up hosting at our own home just once a year. The host would provide the main course; the rest of us would bring sides, drinks, and desserts. Nothing fancy was required.

This monthly "Team Time" lasted just two hours. We'd eat, talk, laugh, hang out, and pray for each other. Then I'd go over a few essentials, share reminders of an upcoming event or retreat, and usually incorporate a small time of training.

And my leaders didn't loathe these "meetings"—*they loved them.* I think they especially loved the bonding.

➲ A VOLUNTEER'S PERSPECTIVE *Danette Matty*

This is so true! We've worked hard on our team for these relational values for the very reasons Jonathan states here!

Do you provide a time like this where your leaders can connect with each other?

Here are some other fundamental ideas and creative twists for your meetings:

- Always involve food. Have your meetings at your favorite pizza place or ice cream shop. Meetings are always better with food!

- Recruit your students' families to host your leadership meetings. Ask the parents to cook dinner for your staff, and then halfway through the meeting, have them come in and share an encouraging story of how volunteer leaders have made a difference in their teenager's life. Maybe have the teenager come in and share what he or she likes about the ministry.

- Highlight a different volunteer each meeting and have the other team members share something they like about that highlighted volunteer. If you're at a restaurant, have everyone help pay for that person's meal.

- Do fun "team-building" games where volunteers work together to solve something.

- Share "wins" and prayer requests. Wins are stories of how God worked through the ministry. These stories give hope and encouragement to team members who are discouraged or are ministering to difficult people. Then lift up these prayers and praises together.

Don't settle for dull meetings. Use it as a time for fun, encouragement, and team-building for your entire ministry team.

→ A VOLUNTEER'S PERSPECTIVE *Danette Matty*

Can I be blunt, youth pastor? Don't waste my time.

Make it worth it for me to show up. Leaders' meetings should be more than just getting the agenda for the next month. Feeding me is a nice perk, but you tell me my leadership is a worthy investment by the quality of your preparation for the meeting.

Don't overwhelm me with a long list of things we need to cover. Go over only the most important events, needs, and communication points; clarify your expectations; and lead a training segment that helps me be a better youth worker.

Some ideas:
- *How to interact with teenagers*
- *How to lead small groups more creatively or effectively*
- *Understanding my own soul care*

And don't forget to add...

4. PERKS

You read it right—perks! These are all the little fringe benefits that we can provide for our volunteers to help them and let them know how much we appreciate them.

Think you can't afford to do this? Actually, you can't afford *not* to do this. Perks are pennies compared to the hours your team members save you, as well as the investment they make in young people's lives.

So when you're budgeting events, make them free for leaders. Here's an example. If you're taking students to a place that costs $8, charge $10 or $12 so you can cover gas costs and pay for volunteer leaders' admission. Most students (or families) that can come up with $8 can come up with a few bucks more.

Plus, many recreational facilities will let in adult "chaperones" (I don't like that word, but these facilities use it) for free.

The key is letting your volunteer leaders know how much you appreciate their time and dedication.

I've been on countless camps and retreats where leaders were required to come up with their own money to cover their costs. This was a financial hardship for many of them—and for many it was a subconscious message that they weren't valuable.

I also gave volunteers additional perks—usually rewarding them for *stuff I wanted them doing*. For example: On my weeklong trips, I wanted leaders to spend time with students one-on-one. So every morning

I gave each leader an envelope with $5 in it. I told them to find a time that day to take a student out for a milkshake or fries and a Coke (or "pop" for you in Michigan). On one trip, I had eight staff on a six-day trip, and they each had about five or six students in their small groups. That meant a total of 48 envelopes with $5 in each, for a grand total of $240.

Sound like a lot? Well, that $240 guaranteed that all 48 students would get one-on-one attention from an adult for about a half-hour. That's more than a lot of them got at home in a week.

Best $240 I ever spent. I just put it in the budget. But at times, my budget was small—I was starting at $0. This meant making a few phone calls to some amazing givers who were willing to finance something like this.

Other perks might be shirts or sweatshirts, a pocketful of game tokens when you go to an arcade, a Starbucks card for taking kids out for a coffee, or Christmas gifts at a volunteer leaders' Christmas dinner.

Providing perks for volunteers lets them know that you value them. The Bible says that where your treasure is, your heart will be also (Matthew 6:21). Our heart needs to be in our volunteers—they could be doing something else with their time.

⊙ A VOLUNTEER'S PERSPECTIVE *Danette Matty*

Let me share some of my thoughts on perks and the investments you can make in your volunteers...

Every summer our youth ministry takes a four-week hiatus from our weekly program. The day after the final youth group gathering before the break, our youth pastor takes students and leaders to a big amusement park a few hours away. Year after year, it's a great memory maker for kids and youth workers.

Our youth pastor always pays leaders' admission. Pay for me to build relationships with teenagers outside of youth group and go on my favorite rides—roller coasters?!? That's a fun perk!

And during that summer break, some leaders and kids get together on their own for sand volleyball, ice cream, or Frisbee golf. If your church does this, help your volunteers see how real-world youth ministry happens outside of programming! Give them ideas they can use to stay connected with students.

But also remember that perks aren't just food, gift books, and roller coaster rides from you. For volunteer Latrice, being part of students' lives and enjoying friendship with other volunteers are true perks. (She's more spiritual than I am. Keep tossing snacks at me; I'll keep showing up.)

Another volunteer, Joe, invited Dan to check out our youth ministry because "the kids are awesome" and he wanted Dan to meet fellow youth leader Cody. Dan later said, "Joe invited me go; God asked me to stay." Two definite perks for Dan: "Being surrounded by students and leaders who want to see Jesus move in our city, and some of the best friends I have come from our youth ministry."

Our youth ministry also provides books for volunteers, which is a way of saying, "We take your leadership development seriously; we don't want to just use you."

For small group leaders we give 99 Thoughts for Small Group Leaders *(Joshua Griffin, Group/Simply Youth Ministry, 2010).*

Here are some other resources we've given our volunteers:

- 99 Thoughts for Youth Workers *(Joshua Griffin, Group/Simply Youth Ministry, 2009)*

- 99 Thoughts for Smaller Church Youth Workers *(Stephanie Caro, Group/Simply Youth Ministry, 2011)*

- 99 Thoughts for Volunteers *(Danette Matty, Group/ Simply Youth Ministry, 2012)*

- Middle School Ministry Made Simple (*Kurt Johnston, Standard Publishing, 2008*)

This year I'm taking a group of volunteers through Jonathan's book Do They Run When They See You Coming? Reaching Out to Unchurched Teenagers (Youth Specialties, 2004). I plan to charge each volunteer a meager $5 (well below retail) just to get the book into their hands as we talk through the ideas and put into practice what we're learning as a team.

In addition to all these elements, once a year I like to have a...

5. LEADERSHIP RETREAT

A leadership retreat really is another perk for volunteers, combined with a great excuse to train leaders and equip them our ministry.

Every summer I concentrated on recruiting volunteer leaders. And at the end of each summer I had a mandatory leadership retreat for new recruits and existing volunteers.

My volunteers all knew that one of the expectations of being on my team was attending this fun weekend once a year—and they loved it.

Often I would take them to my cousin's 900-acre ranch to ride horses, ride all-terrain vehicles, shoot guns, and just have a good ol' time. Not only was the weekend free and fun, but I also made the weekend attractive by encouraging them to bring along their spouse or significant other. This gave them all a chance to interact and bond.

We spent a lot of time doing team-building games or activities, sharing with each other, and just hanging out together. Each person took turns sharing their testimony during the weekend (something they would do in front of kids later that year), usually followed by tears and lots of hugging. Then I did some basic training in evangelism, discipleship, and ministry methods.

Leaders came home from this trip not only trained and equipped, but also as "a team." **Many times I would leave with 15 individuals and come back with one team!**

* * *

Our volunteers are valuable assets. We need to invest in them so that they can invest in students. This can be accomplished through *time, communication, regular "team time," perks,* and *an annual retreat.* Incorporate these five elements and hold on to your ministry team.

7 WAYS TO ENERGIZE YOUR VOLUNTEERS

My dad recently posted a fun little article on his website (VolunteerPower.com) highlighting specific ways to build into volunteers and make them feel special. These ideas were way too good to leave out of this book, so with his permission, here are seven ways to energize your volunteers!

1. Call two volunteers every week. That small effort will provide 104 conversations with volunteers each year. Tell them specifically how much you appreciate their expertise, time, and service. Ask if they're happy with the way things are going and if there's anything you can do to help them.

2. Be visible. Issue press releases about what your church or organization is doing. Give the church body an opportunity to see how God is making a difference through your volunteers. The goal of being visible isn't to get volunteers; it's to let your volunteers know that they're part of something significant.

3. Offer volunteers a benefit for any new volunteer that they bring to one of your events to help in some way. Look at this as the first "date" with a pre-volunteer.

4.   Avoid spending time with draining people who always whine but never do anything. This will free up time to call all your volunteers.

5.   Keep a journal. Write down all the things you do in a day to encourage volunteers. Watch the list grow daily.

6.   Treat special volunteers well. Write a thank you note with a gift certificate for something they would love. Let them know that they're appreciated. If you have the budget, take them to the best restaurant in town. If finances are tight, bake cookies or spend $5 on each person at the local coffeehouse—great treats that still say, "I was thinking about you and appreciate you."

7.   Analyze your retention rate. Have someone on your team build a database that tracks the last time someone quit volunteering with you. The moment someone has a rhythm change, call that person! If someone volunteers in your office every Monday, call that person on Tuesday if he or she didn't show up.

What are you doing to keep your volunteers?

In the next chapter we'll peek at one more vital practice that will help us equip our volunteers...

→ A VOLUNTEER'S PERSPECTIVE *Danette Matty*

To strengthen your ministry, recruit older adults to sponsor an event with resources and prayer. Send them a handwritten note sharing how their gift and prayers impacted the teenagers at the event. Many senior adults have the resources but not the energy to spend with young people. They're happy to support your students, though, and your genuine gratitude encourages ongoing buy-in, both spiritually and materially.

Or have older, caring adults pray for specific students throughout the year. Provide blank cards and stamps for them to send encouraging notes. It's a small effort for the adult, with a big impact for the teenager.

THE SKINNY

ON

VOLUNTEERS

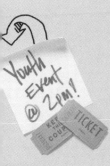

CHAPTER ④

Training

Volunteers

THE SKINNY

ON

VOLUNTEERS

My first year of full-time youth ministry was unique—I wouldn't wish it on anyone. I worked for a struggling organization that provided very little training. As a result, most of what we learned was through the "school of hard knocks"—a nice way of saying we made our share of mistakes.

I remember one of my early events where we shared Jesus with a bunch of teenagers. I told them, "If you'd like to talk with anyone about this, come up front," and a handful of students came forward.

I hadn't planned on this, so I asked a couple of my fresh volunteers if they would come up, too, and talk with these kids. Three volunteers came up to help me, including my friend Paul, who had just started volunteering the week prior.

Paul sat down with a 13-year-old and asked him, "So why did you come forward?"

The teenager pointed at me and said, "Because of what he said."

Paul paused and said, "OK—so, what would you like to do?"

The kid said, "I don't know. He just said come forward."

Paul looked up at me and said, "Jonathan, neither of us knows what to do."

Do you ever have the feeling that Satan is just laughing at us?

I walked away from that moment realizing, *We need to be prepared when a teenager is interested in putting his or her faith in Jesus.*

As it turned out, that kid really was interested in Jesus; he just didn't know how to express it. And my volunteer Paul was really interested in telling him about Jesus, but he didn't know how to verbalize it.

This is where good training is important.

Our volunteers need some basic youth ministry training. Whenever I recruited a new volunteer, I provided a fun training where we taught important topics:

- Understanding the World of Teenagers

- Connecting With Teenagers

- Discovering Doorways of Dialogue About Stuff That Matters

- Sharing Jesus

- Discipling Followers of Jesus

One of the best ways to train volunteers is to take them to a youth ministry conference where they can hear from authors and speakers who are talented communicators and have been in the trenches of youth ministry for decades. Yes, some of these will require a budget, but many churches, organizations, or seminaries will offer free trainings in their area. Keep your eyes open for these opportunities. Get plugged into local youth ministry networks where you can hear about these.

But some conferences can mean big costs. So how can we train our leaders ourselves?

⊙ A VOLUNTEER'S PERSPECTIVE *Danette Matty*

I'm not a big fan of ambiguity—as in, "If you're interested in helping with (name of project or program element), let me know." Or the vague, "I could use someone to do (name of project or program element)."

In your leadership meetings, you might give stirring talks that persuade volunteers to believe in this generation. You're, no doubt, an UH-MAZING person to serve with. But when the meeting ends, I need to know WHAT YOU EXPECT ME TO DO.

Concrete, clearly communicated expectations trump vague wishes and inspire confidence in your leadership.

THE TOP 5 TRAINING METHODS YOU CAN DO YOURSELF

These training and equipping ideas are some of the easiest, cheapest, yet most effective training methods you can incorporate into your ministry calendar.

1. ARTICLE/BOOK DISCUSSION

Training your leaders can be as simple as handing out a book or an article and discussing it as a team.

Just grab an article from your favorite youth ministry magazine or blog and print it out for everyone. At your weekly or monthly gathering, give everyone a copy and have them spend five minutes reading it right there (*if you send it to your team in advance, some won't read it*). Then ask five or six questions about the article.

For example: Take a blog post about youth culture, and the attitudes and trends of teens today, such as a post I wrote about "selfies" (you can access all of my resources through TheSource4YM.com). After your team reads this article, you could ask these kinds of questions:

- Why do so many of our students take selfies?

- How many of us take selfies?

- Do selfies create any risks for us or for our students? If so, how can we address those risks?

- What are some of the struggles we are seeing with self-esteem in our group?

- What can we do about it?

Look for articles that address issues your teenagers are encountering or skills your team needs to practice. And always use these training opportunities to encourage leaders to connect with students and be a positive mentor in their lives.

One nice aspect of this training method is the minimal amount of prep time required. You just need to *(1) find an article and read it,* and *(2) prepare five or six questions.*

The less you talk, the better. This method is more *facilitating* than *speaking*—more *listening* than *lecturing*. You might also learn quite a bit from the knowledge and experience shared by your ministry team.

You can do the same with books, one chapter at a time. I've trained dozens of teams that have read through my book *Connect*. The youth pastor bought the book for each volunteer (a perk), they read a chapter each week/month, and they got together to discuss it briefly. At the end of the year the youth pastor brought me out to do a training workshop on connecting with the different types of kids they encounter in their ministry.

2. SKILL SHARPENING

Our adult leaders often need training in some basic but essential skills, including evangelism, discipleship, leading small groups, and connecting with teenagers. We can train them in these vital skills.

For many of us, this begs the question: *What training material will I use?*

If you have a budget, you'll find some great curriculum options for training volunteers on sharing your faith, leading small groups, and other youth ministry skills. But you also can find some great free options online.

Perhaps you're ready to start developing training material on your own using the skills and tips that you've learned over the years. Try this. Brainstorm *"The Five Ways to Make Kids Feel Heard in Your Small Group."* Or reverse it and train how NOT to do something—always a fun way to teach. Brainstorm *"The 5 Ways to Destroy Your Small Group!"*

Be creative, engaging, and interactive as you teach these topics. Use lots of stories and examples, and focus on getting your team members talking, instead of lecturing at them.

3. THE DEBRIEF

Meet together as a leadership team after a specific activity or event and talk about what you all liked and disliked. If you meet once a month for your "team time," incorporate some quick 5- to 15-minute debriefs after your regular venues: Sunday morning, small groups, a special event—or all of the above.

Or do these "on the spot." Obviously, some larger events might leave people exhausted, so wait a day or two for this debrief—but the sooner the better.

Bringing your team together to discuss what you can learn from each experience gives your team members a chance to be heard, and it will help them learn from each experience and take that knowledge into the next activity or event.

4. BIG-PICTURE PLANNING

Once or twice a year, gather all your adult leaders and plan out the annual calendar. This creates ownership of your various ministry venues and keeps everybody informed about the plans for the full year.

Look at the vision or purpose of your group and then put feet to that purpose. Instead of just doing Wednesday nights, ask your team, "Why do we do Wednesday nights?" or "What do we want to accomplish on a Wednesday night?"

These planning venues should start broad as you ask big-purpose questions, and then eventually get down to "How do we accomplish that purpose each week?"

5. LEADERSHIP RETREAT

Some of the best training times happened when I took my team away for a weekend (like the weekend I described in the previous chapter). On weekends like that, you can do some of the big-picture team training we just discussed.

Don't over-plan the activities at these weekends. Include plenty of hangout time. The top goal should be fellowship. Plan some team-building activities and some training, but make "bonding" your priority.

⊖ A VOLUNTEER'S PERSPECTIVE *Danette Matty*

One of my favorite training experiences was a two-day youth ministry retreat about an hour from where I live. We began each day at 10 a.m., letting tired youth workers sleep in and take their time getting ready.

Therein lie two great tips for your leadership retreats:

- *Choose a location far enough to feel like you "got away" but close enough to drive without feeling wiped out on arrival and return*

- *Allow for a leisurely morning*

You can include early-morning activities as options if you have leaders who are willing to facilitate them. But don't begin the scheduled components until later in the morning. Providing strong programmatic elements—fun team-building activities, meaningful worship experiences, and good speakers—means you won't waste anyone's time or money.

When people return home, they'll feel refreshed, equipped, and inspired.

⊙ A VOLUNTEER'S PERSPECTIVE *Danette Matty*

You've asked the right people, then interviewed, trained, retreated, and "perked" them. But you didn't keep them. Either they chose to leave or you realized they weren't as good of a fit as you'd thought. What do you do?

An "exit interview" can give you insight and help you better shepherd the rest of your team. Even if you don't agree with your exiting volunteer's feedback, you can benefit from understanding their impression of your leadership and ministry.

Sometimes there's nothing you did wrong. But knowing you're willing to hear them will make a difference in the closure these volunteers experience.

Here are some questions to ask, depending on the person's reason for leaving:

- *What did you enjoy about our youth ministry?*

- *How could I have helped you feel more a part of our team?*

- *What would have made your experience more fulfilling?*

- *How can I be praying for you as you transition from the team?*

* * *

Don't underestimate the importance of training your volunteers for ministry. They will appreciate how you equip them to make an impact in the lives of young people.

You have the resources to do this. *(I know you do— because I just gave you a bunch of ideas!)* It's up to you to make the time.

THE SKINNY

ON

VOLUNTEERS

CHAPTER

5

What

Now?

Hello!

THE SKINNY

ON

VOLUNTEERS

A few years ago my friend Stephen called me up with a sound of desperation in his voice. "Jonathan, our school year kicks off in just two weeks, and I'm in desperate need of small group leaders! Who do you know that might be a good volunteer for our ministry?"

Stephen was the youth pastor at our church, and one of my kids had gone through his program. Stephen was sharp, professional, and typically very organized.

We attended the same church, so Stephen was hoping I'd have some names for him. I actually thought of one right away.

"How about Robert, the wrestling coach?" I proposed.

I reminded Stephen a little bit about Robert. I had introduced the two of them a year earlier. Robert attended our church and had a son who was about to enter Stephen's youth ministry.

"There's a hitch," I warned Stephen. "Robert is super busy and is committed in several other areas. I think he'd eventually do it, but to be honest, you need to take it gradually. Just invite him to lunch and pick his brain about his wrestling program and glean some of his knowledge about kids today. Then invite him to come out to an event and help in a small way; he'd for sure do that. Just give him a taste, and Robert will most likely want to eventually join."

Stephen sighed into the phone. "Who else you got?"

I was shocked. "What do you mean, 'Who else have I got?' Robert is golden!"

"He sounds great, Jonathan," Stephen explained, "but I need volunteers now. Who've you got that I can get now?"

A LESSON FROM FARMING

One truth about farming: You can't produce a crop overnight.

Think about it. Let's say you were a farmer and one day a friend called you up and asked you, "I want to grow corn. How do we get some? We love corn!"

You, in your infinite farming knowledge, would talk about how to prepare the soil, plant the seeds, and water the ground. You might even go into great depth about weather and pests and how to prepare for each. Then you'd explain exactly when to harvest and the numerous tools it takes to yield a crop of corn.

Imagine if after explaining all of that, your friend replied, "But I want the corn to grow now!"

Ridiculous, right?

Farming just takes time.

Dating takes time.

Recruiting and equipping volunteers takes time.

Yes, you might be slammed right now with more on your plate than you can handle. You might need 20 volunteers today! But the fact is, volunteers take time. Your work today is probably going to yield results next month, next quarter, and next year. That's just the way mobilizing volunteers works.

That's often just the way *life* works.

AN EYE ON THE FUTURE

The question we all need to ask ourselves: **Do I want to pay my dues now and slowly start reaping the rewards—or do I want to just keep trudging away by myself?**

When I was a kid I pushed my lawn mower all over the neighborhood and offered to mow lawns for $8 a week. After a few weeks I had four customers. Every Saturday I'd push my mower to all four houses and mow their lawns, front and back. It took me a good portion of the day.

The reward of all this hard labor was money in my pocket—quite a lot of money compared to many of my junior high friends. I always had money to spend, and I spent every dime!

I had a friend with similar aspirations, but he didn't spend the money—he saved it instead. After about a year, he went to Sears and bought a riding lawn mower. Then he more than doubled the number of houses he mowed and made three times the money.

Plus, he got to ride that really cool lawn mower—*like a boss!*

For that initial year we were both pushing our mowers, but I was living for the moment, while he was living for the future.

I kept pushing my mower and spending everything I earned.

He paid his dues for a year, set his eyes on the future, pushed his mower every week, and eventually invested in a tool that paid off lavishly.

Which worker are you?

WHAT'S NEXT?

So what can we do right now? Here's what the process looks like.

1. Start by getting on your knees and praying to the Lord of the harvest, "Send me workers."

2. Get out a piece of paper and list out your "dream team." Who has a heart for God and a heart for teenagers and would be awesome additions to your ministry team? Write down their names. Don't stop until you get more names than you want.

3. Pick the perfect first "date" for inviting some of these people and giving them a taste of your ministry.

4. ASK. Invite them to your first "date." Don't invite everyone at once. You want to devote time to them while they are there and invest in each one of them. Give them a taste of your ministry, but also listen to them. Notice their reactions. Don't try to close the deal this night.

5. ASK them to a second "date." "Can we get together for lunch?" Find a time when you can connect, listen, and try to discover their passion

and abilities. Determine if their passion fits your ministry, and if so, where. (If they are the opposite gender, take someone else with you.)

6.   ASK them on a third "date." Invite them to yet another ministry venue—one that you think fits well with their passion.

7.   ASK them to be involved in your ministry. Explain why you want them and talk about how they could make a difference. Incorporate what you learned about their passion and abilities.

8.   If they say yes, then help them through the same logistical process that you need to take all your volunteers through. Even if you know them, background checks and fingerprinting are essential.

9.   Once they're your volunteers, invest in them through your time, communication, perks, and regular equipping opportunities. They are valuable assets worth keeping.

10. Train them and equip them for the work of God's kingdom.

So what are you waiting for? The harvest is great, but the workers are few...